Happy Birthday Mrs. Graves!

You are such a very special lady and you inspire me so much.

Wishing you many more birthday's to come.

God bless you!

Valenda Brock

Especially For

_____

From

_____

Date

_____

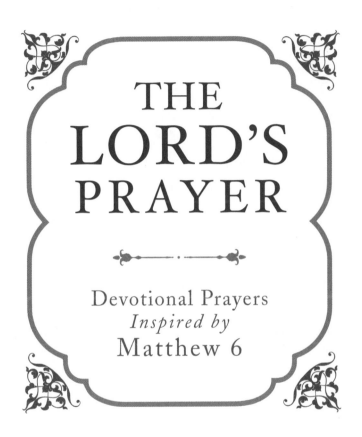

THE LORD'S PRAYER

Devotional Prayers
Inspired by
Matthew 6

BARBOUR
PUBLISHING

© 2013 by Barbour Publishing, Inc.

Special thanks to contributing author Ellyn Sanna.

Print ISBN 978-1-62836-639-6
Special Edition 978-1-63058-337-8

eBook Editions:
Adobe Digital Edition (.epub) 978-1-62416-415-6
Kindle and MobiPocket Edition (.prc) 978-1-62416-414-9

All scripture quotations are taken from the King James Version of the Bible.

Published by Barbour Publishing, Inc., P.O. Box 719, Uhrichsville, Ohio 44683, www.barbourbooks.com

Our mission is to publish and distribute inspirational productsoffering exceptional value and biblical encouragement to the masses.

 Member of the
Evangelical Christian
Publishers Association

Printed in China.

Contents

The Lord's Prayer

Our Father which art in heaven,
Hallowed be thy name.
Thy kingdom come,
Thy will be done in earth,
as it is in heaven.
Give us this day our daily bread.
And forgive us our debts,
as we forgive our debtors.
And lead us not into temptation,
but deliver us from evil:
For thine is the kingdom,
and the power,
and the glory,
for ever. Amen.

MATTHEW 6:9–13

When the disciples asked Jesus how they should pray, He replied with the words of what today we know as the "Lord's Prayer." Most of us are so familiar with the words that we may say them automatically, forgetful of what they actually mean. However, if we look at these familiar phrases more carefully, if we ponder them and pray over them, we will find a deeper understanding of those things Jesus counted most important in our relationship with God. These are words to take seriously and consider intimately. They have the power to transform our lives!

Our Father in Heaven

(HE IS GOD AND I AM NOT)

*J*esus tells us that God is our Father: we are intimately related to the Creator of the universe. Like all good fathers, God loves us; He provides for us; He watches over us.

When we truly believe this, then we can let go of our fears for the future. Our loving Father holds all the details of our lives in His hand. We don't need to worry about money. . .or health. . .or how we will handle our lives' many challenges. Instead we can turn in love and trust to our Father, knowing He can do all things.

As teens, we wanted to break away from our parents, we wanted to prove our independence; this is a healthy developmental stage. But when we are spiritually mature followers of Christ, we can let God be God, and accept that He is in control.

And then we can rest in His love.

Daddy

And because ye are sons,
God hath sent forth the Spirit
of his Son into your hearts,
crying, Abba, Father.
GALATIANS 4:6

*H*uman fathers sometimes let us down. No matter how great (or not-so-great) my own dad is, he is a flawed individual. But You, Father God, always love me, always understand me, always know what's best for me, always provide for me, always keep Your promises. Thank You so much that I can come to You and call You Daddy. Help me to understand that relationship more each day.

Everything Is Possible

*Abba, Father, all things
are possible unto thee.*
MARK 14:36

How amazing, Lord—my Father is the
Creator of the universe! Your infinite creativity
formed the beauty of the earth and the intricacies
of life. I know I can rest assured in Your strength,
in Your might, in Your abilities. There's nothing
on heaven or on earth that You can't handle.
Forgive me when I try to take things into my own
hands. Since You made the world and everything
in it, I know You can take care of my small life!

Joint-Heirs with Christ

*For ye have not received the spirit
of bondage again to fear; but ye
have received the Spirit of adoption,
whereby we cry, Abba, Father.
The Spirit itself beareth witness
with our spirit, that we are the
children of God: And if children,
then heirs; heirs of God,
and joint-heirs with Christ.*
ROMANS 8:15–17

Thank You, Lord, for adopting me into
Your family, for making me Your heir, just as
Jesus is. There's nothing I can do to deserve
this favor or this acceptance. Your grace is
all-sufficient. I now call Jesus my brother, and
together we share in Your amazing glory!

Receiving Jesus

*But as many as received him, to them
gave he power to become the sons of God,
even to them that believe on his name.*
JOHN 1:12

Lord, I believe in Your name. Help me every
day to believe still more. Take away the doubts
and insecurities that the world shouts at me every
day. Keep my eyes firmly focused on You, even
when troubles come. Keep my ears attuned to
Your voice, especially when I am tempted to listen
to other voices. I welcome You into my heart—
to make a home there now and forever.

The Lord Almighty

*And I will. . .be a Father unto you,
and ye shall be my sons and daughters,
saith the Lord Almighty.*
2 CORINTHIANS 6:17–18

*Y*ou, God, can do all things, for You are almighty, all-powerful. Because You are my Father, I know I can trust You to handle each and every aspect of my life. Show me new ways that I can rely on You to work in a mighty way in my life. I trust You with my past, my present, and my future. You are God, and I am not— and I am thankful that's the way it is.

A Father's Mercy

*I will be his father, and he
shall be my son: and I will not take
my mercy away from him.*
1 CHRONICLES 17:13

Thank You, Lord, that You will never take
Your mercy away from me. No matter how many
times I let You down, I can always count on
You to pick me back up. I cannot understand
this gift, but I am thankful for it, Father.
Please show me ways to extend mercy to others in
my life—especially those whom the world
may deem as "unlovable." Because the truth is,
God, I know that most days I, too, am unlovable.

God of All Comfort

*Blessed be God. . .the Father
of mercies, and the God of all comfort.*
2 CORINTHIANS 1:3

You comfort me, Father, when my heart aches.
When everything in my life seems to be going
wrong. . .when the world is full of violence
and disaster. . .when loss is everywhere I look. . .
when hope is dying inside me, Your comfort
never fails. Thank You for offering me that
constant care in my life. Help me to always
extend comfort, care, and compassion to others
as well—ultimately leading them to You.

What Manner of Love

Behold, what manner of love the
Father hath bestowed upon us,
that we should be called the sons of God.
1 JOHN 3:1

A good father protects his children;
he loves his children unconditionally;
he understands and forgives his children;
he provides for his family; he is intimately
involved in the lives of those he loves.
You are more than a good father, God—
You are the perfect Father. Remind me,
Lord, that this is the way You love me.
Thank You for loving all of me—
unconditionally and without reservation.

Lights

That ye may be blameless and harmless,
the sons of God, without rebuke, in the
midst of a crooked and perverse nation,
among whom ye shine as lights in the world.
PHILIPPIANS 2:15

*L*ord, I am grateful that I can claim You as my
Father. Because You live in my heart, I am Your
representative to the world around me. Thank
You for using me for Your purpose, and thank You
for filling in the gaps where I am inadequate to
do Your work. Make me Your light in the world
around me, not so I can gain fame for myself
but only to proclaim Your awesomeness.

Children of the Resurrection

Neither can they die any more:
for they are. . .the children of God,
being the children of the resurrection.
<small>LUKE 20:36</small>

*B*ecause I am Your child, I don't need to be afraid of death. You Yourself conquered death and the grave on Easter morning, and You promise me that Your grace will save me from eternal death as well. How amazing and wonderful and humbling!

I am so glad, Lord, for the promise of Your resurrection and the assurance of eternity with You in heaven. Help me to be bold in sharing this wonderful hope with people who have no hope.

Peace

Grace unto you, and peace,
from God our Father.
2 THESSALONIANS 1:2

Thank You, Father, for the gift of Your
peace. Help me to remember that Your peace
is the only true and lasting rest for my soul—
and to always run to You and no other idol
in my life. When troubles come my way,
please give me an extra dose of Your peace.
And when I see others in turmoil, help me
to always be ready with a word and an action
that will help them seek out Your peace.

Spirit-Led

*For as many as are led by the Spirit of God,
they are the sons of God.*
ROMANS 8:14

Father, let Your Spirit lead me in each thing.
Let me always look to You for guidance and
direction. Keep me away from the temptation
of following the paths of other "gods." Make
Your Spirit alive and active in my heart, so that
I might hear Your voice every day, in my every
decision, and in my every action. Forgive me
when I ignore the movement of Your Spirit.
Make Him active in my heart, Lord!

Peacemakers

Blessed are the peacemakers,
for they shall be called the children of God.
MATTHEW 5:9

Dear Lord, teach me that if I want the world to
see me as Your child, then I need to always work
for peace in the world around me. Help me to resist
the temptation to stir up bitterness or anger among
my family, friends, and neighbors. Take away angry,
jabbing words that may well up in the heat of the
moment. Instead, teach me to be a peacemaker—
so that others can't help but acknowledge that
You are living and active within me.

Loving Our Enemies

But love ye your enemies, and do good, and lend, hoping
for nothing again; and your reward shall be great,
and ye shall be the children of the Highest.
Luke 6:35

Heavenly Father, You know I have a hard time
loving some of the people in my life. Some of them
are downright nasty to me. But Your Word says
that You want me to repay evil for good. Remind
me that You ask me as Your child to not only love
my enemies but to also do them positive, active
good, without thought of reward. It's not going to
be easy, Lord, but with Your help, I can do it.

God's Offspring

*For in him we live, and move, and have
our being. . . . For we are also his offspring.*
ACTS 17:28

The world tells me to be independent,
self-sufficient, and to stand on my own two feet.
But the truth is that I am intimately connected
to the Lord of the universe, and I rely on You
for my life, Father. Most days it's a relief that
it's not all on me to handle everything. To put
it another way, You and I are kinfolk, Lord!
I would not exist if it were not for You.

Who Knows?

*Beloved, now are we the sons of God,
and it doth not yet appear what we shall be.*
1 JOHN 3:2

Father, I'm grateful for being Your child in this life. I can't even imagine what that will mean in the life to come! Thank You for the hope You have given to me for now and for an unknown future. Although I don't know all the details of what You have in store, I am thankful I can rest secure, knowing You have it all under control.

Hallowed Be Thy Name

(PRAISE HIM FOR WHO HE IS)

When we "hallow" something, we set it apart. We keep it holy. We consecrate it. So how do we keep God's name holy and set apart?

In ancient cultures, including the one in which Jesus lived when He was on earth, a person's name was the same as the person himself. It was the essence of that person, his complete character, all that he was.

As we ask God to live in our hearts, He becomes part of us. But at the same time, He remains transcendent. When we hallow His name, we recognize that God is neither a pet we keep on a leash nor an imaginary friend we tuck into our pocket. He is greater than we are, far beyond anything our minds can even begin to comprehend.

When we realize this, we regain a healthy sense of perspective. Our own problems are not as big as we thought they were. God is so much bigger than anything our lives hold. He is unknowable, unimaginable.

And yet He loves us. Love is the essence of His character. Love is His name.

God Is Love

God is love; and he that dwelleth in
love dwelleth in God, and God in him.
1 JOHN 4:16

God, let me never forget that You are love—
patient, kind, not envious, not proud, not rude,
not self-seeking, not easily angered, You keep no
record of wrong. You do not delight in evil, but
You rejoice in the truth. You always protect, trust,
hope, and persevere. Your love will always remain.
It is the greatest thing there is. May I always make
my home within You—within Your love.

Wisdom and Might

Blessed be the name of God for ever and ever:
for wisdom and might are his.
DANIEL 2:20

You, Lord, are all-wise. You make the wisdom of the world look like nothing but foolishness. I will never fully grasp the vastness of Your wisdom, but I am thankful to have that strength in my corner. Scripture says that along with being all-wise, You're all-powerful as well. Speak, and the heavens and the earth are at Your beck and call. No matter how powerful we humans think we are, You are the One who holds it all. Today I "hallow Your name" by relying on Your wisdom and might.

The God of Hosts

*For, lo, he that formeth the mountains, and createth
the wind, and declareth unto man what is his
thought, that maketh the morning darkness,
and treadeth upon the high places of the earth,
The LORD, The God of hosts, is his name.*
AMOS 4:13

God, my Father, You formed the mountains
and the wind, the dark of nighttime and
the morning's light, and You lead all the hosts
of heaven. You formed my intricate features
inside my mother's womb. Let me never take
for granted Your limitless creativity. Let me
never forget who You truly are.

Magnifying Glasses

O magnify the LORD with me,
and let us exalt his name together.
PSALM 34:3

Remind me, Father God, that I am called to be
Your magnifying glass. Shine Your light through
me to all the world around me. Move me
out of the way so that it's all You that others see.
My aim is to exalt Your name in everything I
do—in thought, word, and deed. Lead me to
other people who are like-minded so that we can
truly live lives that worship You and only You.

Our Redeemer

As for our redeemer, the LORD of hosts
is his name, the Holy One of Israel.
ISAIAH 47:4

You are my redeemer, Lord—You have saved
me from all that separated me from You. When
I am not holy, You are. When I am trapped in
anxiety and despair, You free me. When I see no
hope of escape from my present circumstance,
You rescue me. When I feel unworthy and stained
beyond all hope of saving, You cover me with
grace. I worship Your name, Your presence,
Your beauty, and Your strength.

The God of Our Salvation

*Help us, O God of our salvation, for the glory
of thy name: and deliver us, and purge
away our sins, for thy name's sake.*
PSALM 79:9

When I start to look to other things for my
salvation—money, prestige, people, possessions—
remind me, God, that You are the only One
who can save me now and keep me safe forever.
Remove the temptations from my life that I am so
quick to turn to when I'm stressed and insecure.
Make me aware of the pitfalls that surround me.
Focus my attention on You and Your Kingdom.

The Glory of His Name

Give unto the LORD the glory due unto his name:
bring an offering, and come into his courts.
PSALM 96:8

Lord, fill me with the glory of Your name.
May I see the splendor and light of Your character
everywhere I turn. When I am burdened, show
me evidence of Your love in my daily interactions
with others and with Your creation. I want to
always be ready with God-filled responses to
people who ask about my hope.

Get Out of Jail Free

Whosoever shall call on the name
of the LORD shall be delivered.
JOEL 2:32

Father, the world tells me there's no such thing
as a free pass. I need to pay my dues, and then
someday I may (if I'm lucky) reap the reward.
And of course my actions have consequences—
the world is quick to remind me of this as well.
But, Father, when I am in trouble—when my soul
is in captivity—remind me that all I have to do is
call Your name. . .and You will set me free.

Majesty and Strength

*And he shall stand and feed in the strength of the LORD,
in the majesty of the name of the LORD his God.*
MICAH 5:4

Lord, I admit that the stress of life and the
burdens of this world often leave me feeling weak
and powerless. But Your name is majesty and
strength. Your name is higher, more powerful, and
far more excellent than anything this world has to
offer me. All I need to do is tap into the power of
Your name, and You promise to sustain me. I can do
all things through You because You give me strength!

Singing God's Name

I will praise the name of God with a song,
and will magnify him with thanksgiving.
Psalm 69:30

God, fill me with Your song today. Orchestrate
within my heart a melody that is truly a joyful
noise, one that will bring gladness to Your heart.
Give me words of praise to You and words of
encouragement for others. Fill my song with Your
peace and Your beauty. Help me to live out that
song every moment, regardless of my circumstances.
May I hallow Your name with singing.

A God of Justice

For I the LORD love judgment, I hate robbery.
ISAIAH 61:8

If I hallow Your name, God, then I need to remember just who You really are: a God of justice. Remind me that You have called me to show the same justice in everything I do. Thank You for being the perfect balance of justice and mercy, of fairness and love. Try as I might, I cannot strike that balance in my life without Your help. Teach me to love justice and strive for justice every day.

Called by His Name

Thy words were found, and I did eat them; and thy word was unto me the joy and rejoicing of mine heart: for I am called by thy name, O LORD God of hosts.
JEREMIAH 15:16

Oh God, not only have You adopted me as Your child, but now You say I also have Your name as my own. You pursued me, You purchased me, You accepted me, You love me. Although I don't deserve the honor of being called Yours, I am so happy to accept the gift. Help me to strive to be worthy of it.

Eating God's Holiness

That we might be partakers of his holiness.
HEBREWS 12:10

Father, I honor Your name by taking my fill each day of Your holiness. Make Your Spirit alive and active in my heart today. Remind me to always seek You through prayer, meditation on Your Word, and simply being still in Your presence. And when I get "too busy" to take the time to spend with You, please invite me back into Your presence. I can't handle life on my own. . .nor do I want to.

Light

*God is light, and in him
is no darkness at all.*
1 JOHN 1:5

*F*ather God, Your name is Light. You have
no darkness in Your character. Your brilliance is
dazzling—brighter than the brightest star and
more beautiful than the most awe-inspiring
celestial display. You are a hope-filled promise of
never-ending illumination. Please shine on me—
and shine *through* me so that others may see the
darkness of this world flee before Your light.

The Rock

The LORD is my rock, and my fortress,
and my deliverer; my God, my strength,
in whom I will trust; my buckler, and the
horn of my salvation, and my high tower.
PSALM 18:2

So many names You have, Lord: Rock, Fortress, Deliverer, Buckler, Horn of Salvation, High Tower. All of them tell me that I can trust You absolutely. All of them tell me You are in control, that You will shield me from danger, that I shouldn't be afraid, that I am safe in Your mighty hand. You will never let me down.

Truth

Lead me in thy truth, and teach me: for thou art the
God of my salvation; on thee do I wait all the day.
PSALM 25:5

Your Son said He was the Way, the Truth, and the
Life. Father, may I always walk in Your truth,
the truth of Jesus. Teach me patience as I wait for You
to move, to act in my life, as I wait for Your return.
Waiting is not an easy thing to do, God. Please give
me the strength to trust in the hope of my salvation
in You. Your truth means everything to me.

Your Kingdom Come,
Your Will Be Done

(SUPPORTING HIS PLANS)

God's Kingdom is already present. Jesus brought to earth God's saving rule; it is alive and real. But at the same time, there is much work still to be done. Peace and justice must embrace. God's saving power must heal and redeem our broken world.

When we pray that God's Kingdom come and His will be done, we are aligning ourselves with God's ultimate plan for our individual lives, as well as for our world as a whole. We are accepting Christ's agenda as our own. We are celebrating God's ultimate triumph, as we look eagerly toward the day when our eyes will see His glory revealed everywhere.

Out of Sight

*And when he was demanded of the Pharisees,
when the kingdom of God should come,
he answered them and said, The kingdom
of God cometh not with observation.*
LUKE 17:20

*F*ather, I can't always see the reality of Your Kingdom in the world around me. Give me eyes of faith. Show me the people who are working for Your goals, and give me opportunity to serve alongside them. Allow me to bring Your Kingdom to the people and places around me that need You most.

Good News

He went throughout every city and village, preaching and shewing the glad tidings of the kingdom of God.
LUKE 8:1

Make me Your ambassador, Lord, carrying the good news of Your Kingdom to everyone I meet today. Give me new opportunities and new relationships that I may not normally notice, so I can reach more hearts for You. Help me to see these individuals through Your eyes, as loved children of God, created in Your image. Give me the right words to say, and open their ears so they can truly understand the glad tidings of Your Kingdom.

Righteousness, Peace, and Joy

For the kingdom of God is not meat and drink; but
righteousness, and peace, and joy in the Holy Ghost.
ROMANS 14:17

Remind me, Father, (because I forget so easily)
that Your Kingdom is not built on the things
of this world. The truth is that Your Kingdom
flies in the face of the things of the world.
Righteousness, peace, and joy are heavenly
attributes that we humans have a difficult time
living out, without Your Spirit to change our
hearts. May I not depend on external reality for
my satisfaction but instead, dwell always in
Your realm of peace and joy.

The Sower

And he said, So is the kingdom of God,
as if a man should cast seed into the ground.
MARK 4:26

God, what does this mean: Your Kingdom is
like a man casting seed on the ground? Does
this mean I can find Your Kingdom everywhere,
scattered throughout our world by Your generous
hand? Give me new eyes to see Your Kingdom all
around me, especially in places I wouldn't expect
to see You. Father, thank You for Your generosity.
Thank You that You do not ever withhold
Yourself but are always giving.

A Mustard Seed

The kingdom of God. . .is like a grain of mustard
seed, which, when it is sown in the earth, is less
than all the seeds that be in the earth.
MARK 4:30–31

Lord, in order for Your Kingdom to grow and
expand, please plant a seed of faith in my heart.
Make my heart a fertile place for that faith to
grow so that my work in Your Kingdom will be
fruitful. Embolden Your Spirit in me so that I
might contribute greatly to Your plans—not for
my glory but for Yours alone, Father.

Like a Child

*Verily I say unto you, Whosoever shall not
receive the kingdom of God as a little child,
he shall not enter therein.*
MARK 10:15

Give me a child's heart, Lord. Create in me
the simple and heartfelt belief that You celebrate
and cherish in Your children. Let me experience
the wonder of Your love and gift of grace.
Help me to share with others, with childlike
exuberance, the hope I have in You. Let me set
aside grown-up worries and live a joyful life,
so that I can enter Your Kingdom.

More Than Just Talk

*For the kingdom of God is
not in word, but in power.*
1 CORINTHIANS 4:20

God, sometimes I talk a good game, but my
heart and actions don't carry it through. Remind
me that Your Kingdom is active and powerful.
It's not just a bunch of talk. It's real and it's here
on earth now. You ask me to help build Your
Kingdom; show me new ways to serve. Give me a
passion for Your Kingdom on earth—and for
Your heavenly Kingdom as well.

Blessed Poverty

Blessed be ye poor:
for yours is the kingdom of God.
LUKE 6:20

*L*ord, make me willing to be poor in this
world so that I can be rich in Your Kingdom.
Give me a spirit of generosity, even giving
beyond my comfort level so that I must sacrifice
my feelings of security. The things of earth are
not the important things, God. I know You will
take care of me, and You promise me an even
greater reward in heaven.

Dead and Gone

Jesus said unto him, Let the dead bury their dead:
but go thou and preach the kingdom of God.
LUKE 9:60

God, help me to let go of the past and look instead to Your future. I know that You hold my past, present, and future in Your hand. I give You all three and I ask You to be my Savior who covers my past sin, lead me in Your will in my present circumstance, and be with me as I move into Your future. May I not be preoccupied with that which is dead and gone; fill my thoughts and conversation with the reality of Your Kingdom in the here and now.

Healing

And heal the sick that are therein, and say unto them,
The kingdom of God is come nigh unto you.
LUKE 10:9

*Y*our Kingdom, Lord, brings healing to those who are sick in spirit, mind, or body. Enable me to carry Your healing to those around me. Keep me accountable; remind me to not just *say* that I will pray for others who are sick but to earnestly and intentionally come to You on their behalf. Help me to see the healing miracles You supply every moment of every day. And remind me to point others to Your goodness in those situations.

Sanctification

*For this is the will of God,
even your sanctification.*
1 THESSALONIANS 4:3

God, Ruler of my life, You want me to be
sanctified—wholly, utterly given to You. I
surrender myself to Your will. I give You my
heart, my family relationships, my friend
relationships, my career, my ministry, my
hobbies, my health. Gently prod me along to
continue to surrender every area of my life to
You—especially the ones that I try so desperately
to take back and control on my own.

Thanks

In every thing give thanks:
for this is the will of God.
1 THESSALONIANS 5:18

King of the Universe, I give You thanks for
all You have given me, every moment of the day.
Thanks for the health You've granted that allows
me to wake up feeling alert and refreshed. Thank
You for the food that nourishes my body to do Your
work. Thank You for the clothes You have provided
to keep me warm. Thank You for work to do so
I may glorify You. Continue to fill my heart with
gratitude so that I may do Your will in the world.

Delight

I delight to do thy will, O my God.
PSALM 40:8

Thank You, God, that Your will is not one of sadness and gloom. I am grateful that You are not a god who relishes seeing Your children suffer. In fact, You take great pleasure in giving good gifts to me! What a joy to know that You think of me in that way! As I learn to live always within Your Kingdom, I am delighted to be able to give back in some small way as I serve You and others.

Forever

And the world passeth away, and the lust thereof:
but he that doeth the will of God abideth for ever.
1 JOHN 2:17

The things of this world never last. I don't
know why I get excited about acquiring material
things. The anticipation is better than the real
thing, which always ends in disappointment. Even
my cravings for this world's things come and go.
Thank You, Lord God, that Your Kingdom is
permanent, and I will dwell there forever. Give
me a passion for eternity with You—payoff that
absolutely will not disappoint!

First Things First

*But seek ye first the kingdom of God,
and his righteousness; and all these
things shall be added unto you.*
MATTHEW 6:33

You understand, Lord, that I have bills to pay,
deadlines to meet, a house to clean, a family to
care for. These things are important, but they
don't have ultimate importance. Remind me
always to seek Your Kingdom ahead of all these
things. Give me a life of balance that is faithfully
committed to Your call. Help me to trust that You
will take care of (and bless) the details of my life.

Patience

*For ye have need of patience, that, after ye have
done the will of God, ye might receive the promise.*
HEBREWS 10:36

*K*ing of my Heart, I want to do Your will. You know
that sometimes, though, I grow impatient and filled with
doubt. I am distracted by the temptations of the world—
money, relationships, power, prestige—that look like
answers to my problems. In my heart of hearts, I know
they will only lead to ruin. Help me to keep going, relying
on You. I know You always keep Your promises.

Give Us Today
Our Daily Bread

(SUPPLY MY NEEDS)

*I*t's a human tendency to try to safeguard the future. We feel more in control if we think we can guarantee that we'll have everything we'll need down the road. There's nothing wrong with insurance policies or savings accounts, but ultimately, none of us can control what the future holds.

In Jesus' prayer, He speaks of "daily bread," not weekly, not monthly, not yearly. Just as God sent the Israelites manna to collect each morning—food that spoiled when they tried to stockpile it for the next day—God promises to give us exactly what we need for the day ahead. Day by day, He meets our needs for physical and spiritual food.

God wants us to depend only on Him, each day of our lives, believing that He will give us exactly what we need.

That's what it means to walk by faith.

Enough

*God is able to make all grace abound toward you;
that ye, always having all sufficiency in all things,
may abound to every good work.*
2 CORINTHIANS 9:8

*Y*ou make me sufficient, Lord—You give
me enough of everything I need—to carry out
Your will. Truth be told, You often supply *much
more* than I need. These blessings are wonderful
surprises that I don't want to take for granted.
Show me ways that I can share Your blessings with
others. You are a good giver, Lord. Thank You.

God's Riches

*My God shall supply all your need according
to his riches in glory by Christ Jesus.*
PHILIPPIANS 4:19

*W*hy should I ever doubt Your ability to give
me what I need, heavenly Father, when You have
such riches? Your bounty is unfathomable, and
You want to share it with me! How humbling!
Help me to remember that everything I call
"mine" is actually Yours. Forgive me when my
heart is hard and unwilling to accept Your riches
in glory. Help me to be open to Your Spirit
as He moves in my heart.

No Wants

The LORD is my shepherd, I shall not want.
PSALM 23:1

Since You are looking out for me—guarding
and guiding me—I have everything I need. You
are the Good Shepherd who supplies everything
to me, Your sheep. Remind me every day that
as a sheep, I cannot see the bigger picture—the
dangers over the hill or the blessings that are
mine to find. Help me to more fully trust the
Shepherd and His plans for me. Give me a heart
of gratitude and a spirit that relinquishes control.
Thank You, Lord.

Seed and Bread

Now he that ministereth seed to the sower both minister bread for your food, and multiply your seed sown, and increase the fruits of your righteousness.
2 CORINTHIANS 9:10

God, You aren't just a sower or a harvester; You're a true farmer. First You plant the seed; then You water it and nurture it, giving me the food and encouragement I need to grow in You. You work tirelessly to reap a bountiful harvest when my heart is full of fertile soil. I want to return the harvest to You, bearing beautiful fruits of righteousness. Keep working on me, farmer God—I am willing.

Like Birds

Consider the ravens: for they neither sow nor reap;
which neither have storehouse nor barn; and God feedeth
them: how much more are ye better than the fowls?
LUKE 12:24

Lord, if You keep track of the lives of birds,
then I know I can trust You to watch over my
own life. May I rest in the knowledge that You
are always looking after me. I know I am worth
much more to You than a bird. And even
though I know I don't deserve it, I thank You
for Your unconditional love.

Priorities

Therefore I say unto you, Take no thought for your life, what ye shall eat, or what ye shall drink; nor yet for your body, what ye shall put on. Is not the life more than meat, and the body than raiment?
MATTHEW 6:25

*W*hen I start to worry over little things, help me to keep my priorities in order, Father God. Give me grace not to make mountains out of molehills. Time and time again, You have proven that You are faithful to take care of me, so what right do I have to worry? Keep my heart steadfast and my footing secure in the knowledge that You hold me in Your hand.

Prayer and Thanksgiving

Be careful for nothing; but in every thing by prayer and supplication with thanksgiving let your requests be made known unto God.
PHILIPPIANS 4:6

Even while I'm asking You for something, Lord, I can already thank You. I know You hear my prayers, and will answer with "Yes," "No," or "Wait." Thank You for often taking care of my needs even before I ask. What a comfort it is that You already know what I need. I can trust You absolutely to answer me in the best way and according to Your purpose.

God's Ears

And if we know that he hear us,
whatsoever we ask, we know that we
have the petitions that we desired of him.
1 JOHN 5:15

Thank You, God, that You are always listening
to me. You never ignore my prayers, no matter
how silly or insignificant I think my words might
be. It's a mystery how You can possibly hear the
requests of all of humankind at the same time,
but You do! And each moment of communication
is important to You. Thank You for being a God
with always-listening ears.

Promises

*Whatsoever we ask, we receive of him,
because we keep his commandments, and do
those things that are pleasing in his sight.*
1 John 3:22

*H*elp me to keep Your commandments and
always live in a way that pleases You, my Lord. I
know Your commandments are not meant to be
a burden to me but to keep me safe from harm,
from temptations, and to allow me to live in the
freedom of Your love. Forgive me for the times I
feel like Your laws are constraining to me.

Persistence!

*Ask, and it shall be given you; seek, and ye shall find;
knock, and it shall be opened unto you.*
MATTHEW 7:7

*M*ay I trust You enough, Lord, to ask You for
what I need—and then to keep asking, seeking,
and knocking, until You answer. Help me not
to grow weary in coming to You in prayer. I
know that You will keep Your promises—that
You hear me and are working in the details of
my life. When I am praying for others, keep me
committed to taking them to You.

Confidence

*Therefore I say unto you, What things soever
ye desire, when ye pray, believe that ye
receive them, and ye shall have them.*
MARK 11:24

Thank You, Father, that I can come to You
in confidence. I am so unworthy to be able to be
given access to You through prayer, yet You delight
in the communication we have. When I bring
requests to You, I want those requests to be things
that are not selfish or outside of Your will. Grant
that my desires are Your desires, Father. I know that
You will always give me whatever I truly need.

Tomorrow

Take therefore no thought for the morrow: for the morrow shall take thought for the things of itself.
MATTHEW 6:34

The truth is that I have no control over tomorrow, Lord. Free me from worries about the future, whether tomorrow or next week or next year. May I rely on You today, so that I can focus on the here-and-now, this moment, and trust You to take care of whatever comes next. I do trust You, Father. Help my actions be evidence to that fact. I yearn for the freedom that comes from being worry-free!

Heart's Desire

Delight thyself also in the LORD; and he shall give thee the desires of thine heart.
PSALM 37:4

Thank You, God, that You created the deepest, truest desires that live within me. You have made me uniquely different from everyone else, and You've given me a desire to live inside Your will. Thank You for the passions and gifts You have given me. Please show me ways that I can use those gifts to be a blessing to You. I'm glad that as I delight in You, I can trust You always to meet the needs of my yearning heart.

Open Up Wide!

I am the LORD thy God, which brought thee out of the land of Egypt: open thy mouth wide, and I will fill it.
PSALM 81:10

Lord, like a baby bird, I will open wide my soul's mouth, knowing that You will always feed me all I need. Open up my heart today, God, and fill it to the brim with just what I need: encouragement, joy, a spirit of servanthood, a passion for the lost, patience, kindness, and a love for others. I'm ready, Father—fill me up!

Satisfied

And the LORD shall guide thee continually, and satisfy thy soul in drought, and make fat thy bones: and thou shalt be like a watered garden, and like a spring of water, whose waters fail not.
ISAIAH 58:11

Even in the midst of life's droughts—when everything seems dry and dead and dusty— thank You, Father, that You continue to water my heart and satisfy my soul. When I see others are in the midst of drought, give me the right words and actions to share Your living water that will keep them from ever being thirsty again.

Hungry Souls

For he satisfieth the longing soul,
and filleth the hungry soul with goodness.
Psalm 107:9

God, my soul gets so hungry for You sometimes. I know that it's not You who has moved away, but the problem is with me. Thank You that You are immovable, unshakable, and always there. Because of this, I know just where to run to find You, to satisfy my longing soul. Give me a firm footing in Your presence so I am not tempted to wander away again. Thank You for being patient with me.

Forgive Us Our Debts

(Cleanse My Sins)

Sin is what separates us from God. It is everything that is broken, everything that goes off course, away from the path that God wants for our lives. Our hearts are naturally inclined to go astray. And when they do, we feel soiled. . .lost. . . poverty-struck. . .miserable. . .ashamed.

But Jesus came to take away those feelings. He came to get us back on track. He is the bridge that spans the divide that sin makes between God and our hearts. No matter how many times we swerve off course, He's always ready to reach out His hand and pull us back.

Rich in Grace

In whom we have redemption through his blood, the forgiveness of sins, according to the riches of his grace.
EPHESIANS 1:7

The world tells me I should be rich in material wealth, Father, but true riches are found in Your limitless grace. Thank You for the richness of Your grace, Lord. Thank You that Your grace is large enough to cover all my past sin, my current sin, and my future sin. That's the kind of rich inheritance I truly desire!

Promises

*This is my blood of the new testament,
which is shed for many for the remission of sins.*
MATTHEW 26:28

*J*esus' blood is the new testament—the new promise You have made to me, Lord. I am not bound by the rules and regulations of the Old Testament law, but instead I have been given amazing freedom! The blood of Jesus is so powerful that I cannot comprehend it, but please help me to always rely on His saving blood that heals all my sins.

Faithful

If we confess our sins, he is faithful and just to forgive us our sins, and to cleanse us from all unrighteousness.
1 JOHN 1:9

*G*od, I confess to You that I have sinned. I have gone astray, away from Your love. Again and again I fall short. It shames me to admit it, but You ask for my confession. Forgive me. Wash me. Bring me home. Thank You that even now, I can rely on Your faithful love. Thank You for the promise that You are faithful to forgive me—not just yesterday and today, but tomorrow as well.

Power

*The Son of man hath power
on earth to forgive sins.*
MARK 2:10

Jesus, no one else has the power to forgive sins like You do. You took the shame of my sins on Your shoulders as You hung on the cross. I cannot understand the immense pain and suffering You endured as You were beaten and ridiculed. You paid for me. You took care of my insurmountable debt. Thank You for Your sacrifice, and thank You for Your power that sets me free from my sins.

God's Name

Help us, O God of our salvation,
for the glory of thy name: and deliver us,
and purge away our sins, for thy name's sake.
PSALM 79:9

I know that my sins make me dirty, God. More than that, my sins separate me from You. But because You are who You are, You make me clean, Lord. You cover me in the blood of the Lamb, and You deliver me from all my sin so that I may dwell in Your presence. It's nothing that I've done on my own. May I always bring Your name glory!

Purged

Iniquities prevail against me: as for our
transgressions, thou shalt purge them away.
PSALM 65:3

I mess up a lot, Father. In fact, sin seems
stronger than me sometimes, dear Lord. It takes
such a steady foothold in my life that I feel
powerless to change. Purge away this tendency
from my heart, I pray. I will focus on You and
Your Word, Savior God, and I know that You will
lead me away from the temptation of sin.

Backsliding

O LORD, though our iniquities testify against us, do thou it for thy name's sake: for our backslidings are many; we have sinned against thee. . . . Thou, O LORD, art in the midst of us, and we are called by thy name; leave us not.
JEREMIAH 14:7, 9

No matter how far along I go in my spiritual walk with You, Lord, sooner or later I always start to slide backward. There are some temptations and situations that will always make me struggle, and I admit that sometimes I succumb to those temptations and sin. And yet You are here with me. Don't leave me now.

Rebellion

To the Lord our God belong mercies and forgivenesses,
though we have rebelled against him.
DANIEL 9:9

*S*ometimes I act like a two-year-old or a
teenager—I want to do what I want to do when I
want to do it. I disregard what I know is right and
good and travel down a dangerous path. Even when
I'm in the middle of the situation, I know I'm doing
wrong. I rebel against Your love, Lord. Thank You
that despite my sheer stupidity, You always forgive
me, even though I don't deserve it. Help me never
to take advantage of Your forgiveness.

Merciful

I will be merciful to their unrighteousness, and their sins and their iniquities will I remember no more.
HEBREWS 8:12

Thank You that You are a merciful God. You don't even remember all the many times I let You down! You truly forgive and forget. Teach me how to show this kind of mercy to people in my life who have wronged me—that I may shine Your light to others in a real and genuine way, with unconditional love.

Delighted in Mercy

Who is a God like unto thee, that pardoneth iniquity, and passeth by the transgression of the remnant of his heritage? he retaineth not his anger for ever, because he delighteth in mercy.
MICAH 7:18

Father, sometimes when I seek Your forgiveness for a sin that I commit over and over again, I assume that while You are still forgiving me, You might be doing so begrudgingly. But the truth is that You delight in mercy! So You delight in forgiving me? What an amazing thought! What would I do without Your mercy?

Blotted Out

I, even I, am he that blotteth out thy transgressions for mine own sake, and will not remember thy sins.
ISAIAH 43:25

God, I'm so thankful that You don't hold grudges. I give You thanks and praise, dear Lord, for You have not only wiped away all my sins but You also don't even remember them! You wipe my slate clean; You give me a new start; You hit the RESET button. You have made me truly free from the past.

Insurmountable Distance

*As far as the east is from the west, so far hath he
removed our transgressions from us.*
PSALM 103:12

Whenever I feel that I'm a hopeless case, that I'll
never be able to rise above the sin that I fall into,
remind me, Father, that from Your perspective,
my soul and my sin might as well be in different
dimensions, separated by an insurmountable
distance. Take away my shame and guilt that I
feel about my past sins, and help me to rest in
the fact that I am completely forgiven.

Behind God's Back

*Thou hast in love to my soul delivered
it from the pit of corruption: for thou
hast cast all my sins behind thy back.*
ISAIAH 38:17

$\mathcal{I}$ have to imagine that if You put something
behind Your back, Creator God, it doesn't really
even exist anymore. You don't want to look at it,
think about it, or even be bothered by it.
Always remind me that this is what You have
done with my sins! I am free!

The Depths of the Sea

He will have compassion upon us; he will subdue our iniquities; and thou wilt cast all their sins into the depths of the sea.
MICAH 7:19

Thank You for Your loving compassion, heavenly Father, that throws my sin to the bottom of the darkest, deepest ocean—never to be thought of again. Take all the selfish urges of my heart and subdue them, so that I may be free to serve You as I long to.

New Clothes

*Take away the filthy garments from him.
And unto him he said, Behold, I have caused
thine iniquity to pass from thee, and I will
clothe thee with change of raiment.*
ZECHARIAH 3:4

Lord, You offer me a brand-new wardrobe to
replace my filthy clothes that are stained with sin.
Forgive me when I wrongfully believe that my dirty
rags are adequate and I try to hold on to them.
Help me to put on the new clothes You hold out
to me. Dress me in Your love and forgiveness.

Showered

*Then will I sprinkle clean water upon you,
and ye shall be clean: from all your filthiness,
and from all your idols, will I cleanse you.*
EZEKIEL 36:25

Each time I take a shower, God, remind me that
You have showered my soul with Your love. As I
lather up with soap that will cleanse the dirt of the
day, remind me of the cleansing power of Your grace
and mercy. You have washed away everything in
me that was false, and now I am truly clean.

As We Also Have Forgiven Our Debtors

(TEACH ME TO FORGIVE)

When someone treats us in a way that seems unfair, we so easily focus on that slight. We brood over it. We talk to others about it. It keeps us awake at night. Even the smallest offenses can grow larger and larger in our minds, the more we think about them. And when it comes to truly large offenses—when someone has hurt a person we love, for example, or when violence is done to innocents in the world—we feel justified in hugging to our hearts our anger and outrage.

But this isn't what forgiveness looks like. Forgiveness sets aside slights, no matter how real or undeserved or huge they may be. Forgiveness imitates the mercy God has shown to our own hearts. It remembers that when God has forgiven us of so much, we can afford to forgive others as well.

Jesus asks us to forgive.

Whenever I Pray

And when ye stand praying, forgive, if ye have
ought against any: that your Father also which
is in heaven may forgive you your trespasses.
MARK 11:25

Whenever I come to You, Lord, asking You to
grant me some request, remind me first to let go
of any unforgiveness I'm holding in my heart. I
don't want to be a grudge-holder, and I know that
withholding forgiveness hurts me more than it
hurts the other person. Show me ways to show true
grace—Your grace—to others who have hurt me.

Anger Deferred

*The discretion of a man deferreth his anger;
and it is his glory to pass over a transgression.*
PROVERBS 19:11

*T*he word *glory* refers to the essence of
something, the quality that makes it give forth
light. Dear God, remind me that I am most truly
myself, my best and shiniest self, when I don't act
on my anger against others. Give me the wisdom
to know how to react to people and situations in
the same way You would react. Let love, respect,
and kindness be at the root of everything I do.

Persecution

Do good to them that hate you, and pray for them
which despitefully use you, and persecute you.
MATTHEW 5:44

*F*ather, bless all those who have hurt me,
all those who have hurt those I love, all those
who have hurt the innocents of our world.
I ask that You show me how to reach out my
hands in kind and practical ways to these
individuals who have brought hurt into our world.
Help me to see past their actions to their own
hurt. Use me to show them Your mercy and love.

Blessings Instead of Curses

*Bless them that curse you, and pray
for them which despitefully use you.*
LUKE 6:28

My Lord, I feel misused. I feel cursed. I feel slighted and abused. I'm angry and hurt. I come to You with these feelings, and I give them to You. Take away the hurt and my desire for revenge. Give me Your heart when it comes to others. I pray that You would bless the people who have made me feel this way. Your will be done, Father.

Inheritance of Blessing

*Not rendering evil for evil, or railing for railing:
but contrariwise blessing; knowing that ye are
thereunto called, that ye should inherit a blessing.*
1 PETER 3:9

*I*t's my first reaction to strike back when
I'm hurt, to complain against people who
complain about me. You know those tendencies
within me, Father. Turn them inside out, I pray,
and may my first reaction instead be always to
pray and bless. When I feel that this is too much
to ask of me, remind me that You will give back
to me countless blessings in return.

Putting Up with It!

<hr />

Being reviled, we bless;
being persecuted, we suffer it.
1 CORINTHIANS 4:12

God, give me patience to put up with all the
grief that comes my way! You know the things
that push my buttons, that get under my skin.
Give me the peace to endure them. I know You
will use the situation according to Your will, but
it's not so fun to suffer through it! Give me the
comfort and encouragement I need to endure.

Feeding My Enemies

Therefore if thine enemy hunger,
feed him; if he thirst, give him drink.
ROMANS 12:20

*I*t's not enough to *forgive* my enemies, Lord;
now You ask me to actively do them good—to do
whatever I can to meet their needs. I'm hurting so
much right now that I can't do this on my own,
Father. Show me how You want me to do that,
and then give me the strength to do it. May I look
for opportunities to help those who have hurt me.

Waiting for God

Say not thou, I will recompense evil;
but wait on the LORD, and he shall save thee.
PROVERBS 20:22

When a situation arises where wrong has been done, I'm quick to feel that the situation is urgent: I have to do something about it *right now*. Teach me, Lord, to wait for You instead. Give me Your wisdom in these situations, and when the time is right, show me what to say and what to do that will bring glory to You.

The Other Cheek

*Whosoever shall smite thee on thy
right cheek, turn to him the other also.*
MATTHEW 5:39

*R*eally, God? If someone hurts me, do I really
have to ask him to hurt me again somewhere
else? That seems like You're asking too much! It
goes against everything society teaches me about
standing up for myself, about being assertive, about
not being a doormat. Teach me what Jesus meant
when He said this. Give me a heart that wants to
follow His example. . .even when I don't want to.

Following Good

See that none render evil for evil unto any
man; but ever follow that which is good,
both among yourselves, and to all men.
1 Thessalonians 5:15

Even when I see evil all around me, Lord, help me
to always follow that which is good rather than evil.
Forgive me when I am lured by the fake shininess
and beauty that evil displays. Keep me from falling
for the tricks of the devil, and keep my feet securely
on Your path, the good and right path.

Love

[Love] beareth all things, believeth all things,
hopeth all things, endureth all things.
1 CORINTHIANS 13:7

Give me a loving heart, God. Help me to endure
hurts, always hoping and believing in the best in
others. Remind me that love is an everyday action,
not just when I feel like it. Help me to show love
in words as well. Give me Your eyes to see the true
worth of the people around me, and help me to
always display Your love to them. Thank You for
being the perfect example of love.

Quarrels

Forbearing one another, and forgiving one another, if any man have a quarrel against any: even as Christ forgave you, so also do ye.
COLOSSIANS 3:13

Quarrels come so easily some days, Lord, especially with the people I live and work with closely. Remind me that Christ has forgiven me for far greater offenses, and help me to bite my tongue before I start an argument. When I do stumble and take part in a fight, help me to be humble and ask for forgiveness from the other person. Grant me freedom in my relationships so I am not distracted by bitterness.

Tenderhearted

*And be ye kind one to another, tenderhearted,
forgiving one another, even as God for
Christ's sake hath forgiven you.*
EPHESIANS 4:32

The world may look at a tender heart as a
weakness, but You know better, God. Your heart
is tender toward me, and You are quick to extend
grace and mercy. Give me a tender heart, I pray.
Guard my heart so that it won't become calloused
to the hurts and evils of the world. Fill me with
Your kindness, gentleness, compassion, and
sincerity, so that I can forgive others just as
I have been forgiven.

Overcoming

Be not overcome of evil,
but overcome evil with good.
ROMANS 12:21

When darkness seems to be attacking me from all sides, Lord, give me Your strength so that I can rise above the world's evil. Make Your Spirit strong in me so that I can feel Your presence near. Give me the words to say and the things to do to bring Your goodness to every situation. Use me in whatever way You can for Your will to be done. I know I'm on the winning side!

God's Children

Be ye therefore followers
of God, as dear children.
EPHESIANS 5:1

$\mathcal{B}$rothers and sisters often bicker and squabble.
My siblings and I are no exception. But remind me,
dear God, that Your children should be following
You, not fighting with each other. Grant us an
abundance of grace when we are dealing with each
other, and help us keep our eyes solely on You as we
work through difficulties. If we are following Your
will, we will be blessed beyond imagination.

Merciful

Be ye therefore merciful,
as your Father also is merciful.
LUKE 6:36

Father, I am so thankful for Your mercy, and I am thankful for Your gift of grace—but You know that it is sometimes difficult for me to show mercy to others. It's especially hard for me to be merciful when I see someone making the same mistake over again or committing the same sin again and again. But right now I pray that You make me like You. Help me to show Your mercy to everyone—with no exceptions.

And Lead Us Not into Temptation

(PROTECT MY HEART AND SPIRIT)

As children, many of us felt confused by this verse in the Lord's Prayer; it seems to indicate that God will tempt us to sin unless we specifically ask Him not to do so. Other translations for the Greek word, however, might be "trials" or "tests."

Life brings to all of us difficult times, times when our faith and strength is tested. Jesus is telling us here in His prayer that during those times, we can ask for God's help and protection. When we are tested, God will help us to pass with flying colors. He will help us escape our times of trials.

Shielded

*Above all, taking the shield of faith, wherewith ye
shall be able to quench all the fiery darts of the wicked.*
EPHESIANS 6:16

$\mathcal{L}$ord, You tell me that my faith is a shield that
will protect me from evil. Right now I ask You to
reinforce that shield. Give me a greater, stronger
faith so that I will be ready when I go through
difficult times, when Satan is shooting his fiery
darts directly at me. I will not live in fear about
this possibility, but I will stand on Your promises.

God's Gentleness

*Thou hast also given me the shield of thy salvation:
and thy gentleness hath made me great.*
2 SAMUEL 22:36

*F*ather God, when I think about Your gift of
salvation to me, I think about the mighty work
that Your grace through the death of Jesus Christ
does in my life. But there's another side to it. God,
thank You for Your gentleness that makes me
strong enough to rise above every trial that comes
my way. It's because I am saved that I can be
free to stand and not be afraid.

God's Armor

*But let us, who are of the day, be sober,
putting on the breastplate of faith and love;
and for an helmet, the hope of salvation.*
1 THESSALONIANS 5:8

Father, remind me not to venture out into life's
temptations and trials without first putting on
Your armor, especially the breastplate of faith
and love and the helmet of Your salvation. Teach
me to grab hold of these gifts and harness the
power that You offer through them. Give me the
opportunity to use these pieces of armor to bless
others, protecting them against the power of evil.

Lit

*Let your loins be girded about,
and your lights burning.*
LUKE 12:35

*W*hen everywhere I look I see only darkness,
please, Lord, turn on the lights in my heart. Show
me ways to share that illumination with everyone
around me. When Your light burns, darkness flees.
Use me. Light me, I pray.

Wide Awake

Therefore let us not sleep, as do others;
but let us watch and be sober.
1 THESSALONIANS 5:6

You know how tired I am, God. You know how weary I am of facing troubles and challenges. Help me not surrender to my exhaustion. Send godly friends into my life that can encourage me to continue on the path that You have laid for Your children. Keep me wide awake and alert, focused always on You.

Delivered

Because he hath set his love upon me,
therefore will I deliver him: I will set him
on high, because he hath known my name.
PSALM 91:14

When troubles threaten to drown me, loving
Lord, reach down and save me. Deliver me from
the floods. Rescue me from the fire. Remove me
from the storm. Protect me from the violence.
Pick me up and set me on a high place where
I will be safe in Your presence.
I know my Deliverer is coming.

Preserved

The Lord preserveth all them that love him.
PSALM 145:20

Preserve me, God; keep me safe—that's what
I'm asking of You. Guard my physical body,
my head, and my heart. Grant me travel mercies
as I move from place to place. Take away my
anxiety, my worries, and my woes. I love You—
and I need Your help now. I can't do it alone.

Alive and Blessed

The LORD will preserve him, and keep him alive;
and he shall be blessed upon the earth: and thou wilt
not deliver him unto the will of his enemies.
PSALM 41:2

Sickness. . .violence. . .exhaustion. . .stress: our
world is full of dangers. Some of the dangers I
face are truly life-threatening, Lord. But I don't
want to live a life of fear. You call me to be bold
and fearless. Thank You that You've promised to
not only save my life but also to bless me.

Never Forsaken

*For the LORD loveth judgment, and forsaketh
not his saints; they are preserved for ever.*
PSALM 37:28

*F*ather God, I've experienced abandonment
in my life. The experience left me feeling empty,
alone, helpless. Thank You, Father, that You will
never forsake me; You will never abandon me.
I am grateful for the security this promise affords
me. You will keep me safe forever in Your loving
arms that are big enough and strong enough to
hold me and all my issues.

Saved from All Evil

The LORD shall preserve thee from
all evil: he shall preserve thy soul.
PSALM 121:7

*E*vil comes in so many shapes and forms.
Sometimes it comes into my life disguised, and by
the time I recognize its presence, my soul is already
in danger. When this happens, Father, be my
rescuer (even when I don't ask for rescuing!). Thank
You, Lord, that You are always watching over me—
and You will protect me from evil of every kind.

My Hiding Place

*Thou art my hiding place; thou shalt preserve
me from trouble; thou shalt compass me
about with songs of deliverance.*
PSALM 32:7

Heavenly Father, when the world seems like
a dangerous place, when anxieties rush at me
everywhere I turn, be my hiding place. Be by my
side and let me run into Your arms. Wrap me up in
Your embrace and sing to me Your sweet song of
deliverance. May I never think I'm so self-sufficient
that I reject Your comfort and protection, Daddy.

A Tower on a Rock

—◆◆ · ◆◆—

The God of my rock; in him will I trust:
he is my shield, and the horn of my salvation,
my high tower, and my refuge, my saviour;
thou savest me from violence.
2 SAMUEL 22:3

*Y*ou, oh Lord, are my place of absolute safety:
a high tower built on a rock that will never move.
When trials and temptations surround me,
teach me to lift my gaze higher. Help me to look
above all my troubles and see Your tall tower—
and then run there as fast as I can!

My Refuge

The LORD also will be a refuge for the oppressed, a refuge in times of trouble.
PSALM 9:9

*I*n times of trouble, Lord, when I feel that the pressure is overwhelming, thank You that You are my refuge—a place of peace, love, and acceptance. Teach me to seek Your protection at the onset of troubles, rather than trying to handle them on my own. I don't get extra points for trying to stick it out by myself.

Singing

But I will sing of thy power; yea, I will sing aloud of thy mercy in the morning: for thou hast been my defence and refuge in the day of my trouble.
PSALM 59:16

God, You know all the troubles that surround me—but today, I'm going to start my day singing. Give me a song of power and mercy that will stay with me all day long, especially when the stresses of the day come. No matter what life throws at me, I want to live with Your joyful melody in my heart until Jesus returns to take me home!

Hope

Thou art my hiding place and
my shield: I hope in thy word.
PSALM 119:114

God, I know that one of the surest ways to find
Your hope is to open up scripture and meditate on
Your Word. There I learn that You thought of me
at the beginning of creation, that You formed me in
my mother's womb, that You love me and cherish
me, that You provided a way for me to have an
intimate relationship with You through the death,
burial, and resurrection of Jesus Christ, and that You
have amazing plans for me here and into eternity.
Your words fill me with amazing hope, Father.

Safe in the Midst of the World

*I pray not that thou shouldest take them out of the world,
but that thou shouldest keep them from the evil.*
JOHN 17:15

Jesus, You didn't ask that I be physically removed
from the earth, so that I'd be immune to the world's
temptations and tests. Instead, You asked that God
protect me no matter what I face. Thank You,
Jesus, that You prayed for *me*.

*But Deliver Us
from the Evil One*

(GUIDE MY STEPS)

*J*esus didn't pretend that there was no evil in the world. Instead, He teaches us in His prayer to focus on God's deliverance. Even when we are surrounded by evil's darkness—even when this life's evil presses so close around we that we can see nothing with our own eyesight—even then, God will guide our steps.

We may not be able to see the path ahead, but God knows the way. He will keep us safe as we continue on life's journey, through the darkest days. We may not always be able to know He is there, but He will never forsake us. And one day, He will lead us safely home.

Yes and No

But let your communication be, Yea, yea; Nay, nay:
for whatsoever is more than these cometh of evil.
MATTHEW 5:37

God, teach me Your ways so that no evil will
take root in my life. Remind me to make my word
count, so that my "yes" means yes, and my "no"
means no. Make me a person of integrity whom
others can trust. When people ask me why I do
what I do, let me always point them to You.

Clothed in Truth

*Stand therefore, having your loins girt about with
truth, and having on the breastplate of righteousness.*
EPHESIANS 6:14

Father, this world has exchanged truth for
lies. What You see as black and white, society
sees as gray. Right and wrong has been twisted
in such a way that many people are confused and
don't even know what to think. Today I ask that
You clothe me in truth, so that I can live as You
want me to. Give me the boldness to stand up for
what is right, and in love guide others to You,
the ultimate source of Truth.

Hope to the End

Wherefore gird up the loins of your mind, be sober,
and hope to the end for the grace that is to be brought
unto you at the revelation of Jesus Christ.
1 PETER 1:13

I have put my hope in Your grace, Lord, which You showed to me through the life of Your Son, Jesus Christ. The account of His death, burial, and resurrection is one that saves me for all of eternity, but meanwhile, I want to emulate His example of grace-filled living now, in my everyday life. Help me to always keep His example as my focus.

Firm

But the Lord is faithful, who shall
stablish you, and keep you from evil.
2 THESSALONIANS 3:3

God, I know You are faithful. Be my rock and
my firm foothold, and please be the foundation
of my life. Make me firm and solid, so that I can
always resist evil. When my own faith is firmly
rooted, then please allow me to help others find
their strength in Your faithfulness. Your strength
will sustain all Your children!

No Slipping

———•———

He will not suffer thy foot to be moved: he that keepeth thee will not slumber.

PSALM 121:3

*I*m coming to a situation in my life where the way ahead looks slippery and dangerous, Lord. Please hold my hand, and when necessary pick me up and carry me. I know that You won't leave me or even take a break to get a little rest. Thank You that I can rest in You, even during difficult stretches of the path.

Straight Ways

*Lead me, O LORD, in thy righteousness because of
mine enemies; make thy way straight before my face.*
PSALM 5:8

*G*od, You know how hard it is for me sometimes
to know which way I should go. Today I ask that
You be my map and my guide. Please show me
clearly the way You want me to follow. Remind
me that You've already been there and done that.
While I may question why we're going a certain
way, You know what is best and You have
great plans for me.

Plain Paths

*Teach me thy way, O Lord, and lead me
in a plain path, because of mine enemies.*
PSALM 27:11

I need Your help, Lord. I can't see which
path I should take. It's dark, I'm confused,
and the enemy of my soul has hidden Your
way from me. Please, Lord, lead me—
and remove the evil that is in the way!

Walking in Truth

Teach me thy way, O LORD; I will walk in thy truth: unite my heart to fear thy name.
PSALM 86:11

I am guilty of having a divided heart, God. I want to do Your will, but I also want my will to be done. Forgive me for my selfishness. When my heart feels torn with conflicting desires, Father God, please unite me, so that I have a single focus in life: Your way, Your truth, Your will, Your path.

Morning Love

Cause me to hear thy lovingkindness in the morning;
for in thee do I trust: cause me to know the way
wherein I should walk; for I lift up my soul unto thee.
PSALM 143:8

It is my desire, Father God, to meet You in
prayer every morning. As I start out each day,
give me ears, loving Lord, to hear Your voice—
and then may I listen for that still, small voice all
through my day. Follow me into the evening and
whisper loving thoughts to me at night as I rest
my head, ready to meet You again in the morning.

God's Eye

*I will instruct thee and teach thee in the way which
thou shalt go: I will guide thee with mine eye.*
PSALM 32:8

I have a dog that follows the direction of my gaze
and knows what I want her to do. All I need to do
is look at her bed for her to go there and lie down;
if I look in another direction, toward a treat I've
hidden for her, she leaps up and runs to the morsel
of food. Lord, help me to be as responsive to Your
gaze. Keep me so tuned in to You that You can use
Your eyes to show me where You want me to go.

For My Own Good

---

*Thus saith the LORD, thy Redeemer, the Holy
One of Israel; I am the LORD thy God which
teacheth thee to profit, which leadeth thee
by the way that thou shouldest go.*
ISAIAH 48:17

Sometimes I forget, Lord, that Your guidance
is always for my good. I admit that sometimes it
feels a little bit like taking my medicine. But You
want what's truly best for me. Your paths always
lead me to joy and blessing and health. Teach me
to trust You more fully today and every day.

Open Ears

And thine ears shall hear a word behind thee, saying,
This is the way, walk ye in it, when ye turn to the right
hand, and when ye turn to the left.
Isaiah 30:21

Give me sharp ears, heavenly Father, so that I can
hear Your voice. Tune my ears to be receptive to only
You, and give me discernment so I can disregard
the false voices that may try to imitate You.

No More Crooked Ways

I will bring the blind by a way that they knew not;
I will lead them in paths that they have not known:
I will make darkness light before them, and crooked
things straight. These things will I do unto them,
and not forsake them.
ISAIAH 42:16

Sometimes my life's path seems to take one unexpected turn after another. I feel as though I'm stumbling through a dark maze. One day, though, Lord, when I look back at my life from heaven's perspective, will I see that You made my life's crooked paths run absolutely straight, right to You?

The Path of Life

*Thou wilt shew me the path of life:
in thy presence is fulness of joy; at thy right
hand there are pleasures for evermore.*

*W*hy do I think I'm a trailblazer, Lord?
Sometimes my way seems better to me,
so I take a little side trip off Your path, only
to find disappointment, destruction, and
heartbreak. I know that only Your path, God,
leads me to life. . .to joy. . .to pleasures that
will last forever. I will put blinders on my eyes,
Father—looking straight ahead to You.

Standing Up Straight

Teach me to do thy will; for thou art my God: thy spirit is good; lead me into the land of uprightness.
PSALM 143:10

My burdens have been feeling extra heavy lately, Father. I am still walking along Your path, but maybe You've noticed my shoulders slumped, my head hung low. Gently remind me that I don't need to carry these burdens—that You are strong enough to carry all the weight of the world. I give You my worries and woes, Father. Help me to stand upright and follow the path of Your perfect will.

Everlasting Ways

*See if there be any wicked way in me,
and lead me in the way everlasting.*
PSALM 139:24

You know, Lord God, how easily I hide selfishness inside my heart. But try as I might, I cannot hide it from You. Shine Your light on all my blind spots. Show me where I need to grow and change to be more like You. Bring true godly friends into my life that can help me in these areas. Lead me in the path that will lead me to eternity.

For Yours Is the
Kingdom and the Power
and the Glory Forever

(PRAYERS FOR MY FUTURE)

We look forward to the future if we think we can predict that it will hold good things, but we dread and fear the difficult things we know lie ahead. We cannot escape death and old age, loss and sorrow. And we fear the unknown, the future we can't predict or control.

But the Lord's Prayer offers us hope. Jesus tells us to pray for today's needs—and then He tells us to rely on God's power for the future. Through Jesus, we are citizens of a Kingdom that will last forever, a Kingdom of light and splendor. Why should we fear the future, when—no matter what it holds—it will lead us higher and deeper into the Father's Kingdom?

Future Glory

*For I reckon that the sufferings of this present
time are not worthy to be compared with
the glory which shall be revealed in us.*
ROMANS 8:18

When it comes down to it, God, it's not all
about me. I am guilty of being so selfish, self-
centered, "me-focused" that I lose perspective of
the big picture. Father God, when pain surrounds
me, give me a glimpse of the glory that lies ahead.
Help me regain a proper sense of perspective.
Show me where You want me in Your will!

Eternal

For our light affliction, which is but for a moment,
worketh for us a far more exceeding and
eternal weight of glory.
2 CORINTHIANS 4:17

When I think about eternity, God, I realize that
the time I spend on earth is pretty insignificant.
But I still get so focused on my daily problems,
Lord, that they seem insurmountable. Burdens
and worries eat away at my joy, Lord. Instead,
I choose to yield myself to whatever comes into
my life and rely on Your power to get me through.
Use my problems and troubles to transform
me for eternity, I pray.

Blessed Hope

*Looking for that blessed hope, and the
glorious appearing of the great God
and our Saviour Jesus Christ.*
TITUS 2:13

Some days, Father, I hold on to a single thread
of hope. But the hope You offer through Jesus
Christ is real and active, and even when it's
wearing thin, it sustains me. The hope I have in
You, God, is for the future—but it blesses me
today. Fortify my hope so that I can share it with
other weary travelers in this world. Help me direct
them to the true source of hope.

When Christ Appears

When Christ, who is our life, shall appear,
then shall ye also appear with him in glory.
COLOSSIANS 3:4

*J*esus, I look forward to Your return to earth. I'm so thankful that I am not on my own—that You are with me all the way. Thank You for the gift of Your Holy Spirit that lives in me and empowers me with the strength necessary to live for God. You are my life now, and You will take me with You into glory, where I will be made perfect.

God's Thoughts

---

*For I know the thoughts that I think toward
you, saith the Lord, thoughts of peace,
and not of evil, to give you an expected end.*
JEREMIAH 29:11

God, You know how easily my thoughts turn
to worries and fears. Teach me to think Your
thoughts instead: thoughts of peace and goodness
that will lead me into the future You have planned
for me. Show me the steps I should take to reach
the abundant life You have in store for me, both
here on earth and in eternity.

Before the World Began

In hope of eternal life, which God, that cannot lie,
promised before the world began.
TITUS 1:2

Think of it, Father! You are a God that cannot lie—there is no falsehood or deceit in You. Your promises are better than gold and they reach forward into eternity—and they reach backward, before the heavens and earth were made. There is no place in time's long arc where You are not, so why should I worry about past, present, or future? Hold me in Your hand today.

God's Riches

O the depth of the riches both of the wisdom and knowledge of God! how unsearchable are His judgments, and his ways past finding out!
ROMANS 11:33

When I start to worry about my life, Father, when I start to feel as though You may not know what You're doing—remind me that Your riches are far greater than my needs. Give me a spirit of peace when I don't understand the whys, secure in my faith that You are doing a good work that will bring glory to Your name.

All Grace

*The God of all grace, who hath called us
unto his eternal glory by Christ Jesus, after
that ye have suffered a while, make you
perfect, stablish, strengthen, settle you.*
1 PETER 5:10

I'm glad, God, that Your grace is so wide and
great that it can work even through this life's
pain and suffering. Give me the right amount
of comfort to endure those times of pain and
suffering, and remind me that in the end, I can
count on You to make me perfect and strong,
settled in Your love forever.

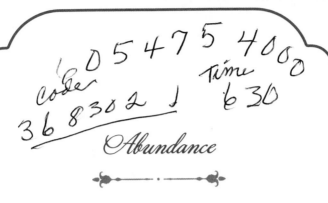

Abundance

*[God] is able to do exceeding abundantly
above all that we ask or think, according
to the power that worketh in us.*
EPHESIANS 3:20

Father, I often put limits on what is possible in
my life—to my own detriment! Help me to recall
the miracles You've done in my life—the "God-
incidents" that have Your fingerprints all over
them. Remind me to share these fantastic stories
with others so they, too, might learn to see You
at work in their lives. Give me Your eyes to see
the endless power You have at work in me. May I
expect Your abundance to fill my future.

Shining More and More

The path of the just is as the shining light,
that shineth more and more unto the perfect day.
PROVERBS 4:18

*F*ather, when I am in vibrant fellowship
with You, the path before me seems clearer
and Your will seems more evident. Thank You
for the light that shines brighter with each step
I take. When the light seems dim or I'm not
sure which way to go, bring me back into Your
presence and lead me to Your holy Word.
Thank You for never giving up on me, Father.

Like Jesus

*Beloved, now are we the sons of God, and it
doth not yet appear what we shall be: but we
know that, when he shall appear, we shall be
like him; for we shall see him as he is.*

1 JOHN 3:2

God, You promise that You're not done with me
yet. In fact, I won't be finished until You come
again to the earth and take me home with You.
It doesn't really matter what my future holds,
God, so long as one day I will be like Jesus.

Face-to-Face

For now we see through a glass, darkly;
but then face to face: now I know in part;
but then shall I know even as also I am known.
1 Corinthians 13:12

You know that I can't see You clearly, Father.
You know I don't really understand You, even
when I am seeking You every day. I'm grateful,
though, that I expect to see You face-to-face—
and that on that day, I will finally truly know You
even more intimately and personally than now.
What an awe-inspiring promise!

Glory to Glory

But we all, with open face beholding as in a glass the glory of the Lord, are changed into the same image from glory to glory, even as by the Spirit of the Lord.
2 CORINTHIANS 3:18

You have given me glory in this world, God. You have given me splendor and light. You have created my very essence so that it shines. And as I keep my eyes on You, You are creating within me even greater glory. May Your Spirit work in my heart, God, so that I am transformed into Your image.

Strength to Strength

They go from strength to strength.
PSALM 84:7

You know the strength I need to face today, Lord. You know the strength I'll need for tomorrow, for next week, for next year. You know what I'll need to face each of the challenges that lie ahead in my life. You know the day of my death, and You know exactly what I'll need on that day, too. So I need not worry about anything. You will lead me from strength to strength, like jumping from stone to stone across a river.

With Jesus

Father, I will that they also, whom thou hast given me, be with me where I am; that they may behold my glory, which thou hast given me.
JOHN 17:24

*G*od, as much as I may wish I knew what the future holds, only You know what will happen. Instead of worrying about things that I cannot control, I want to simply follow You into tomorrow and into eternity. The truth is, I don't really care where You lead me. . .so long as Jesus is there, too.

Joy

*For ye shall go out with joy, and be led forth
with peace: the mountains and the hills shall
break forth before you into singing, and all the
trees of the field shall clap their hands.*
ISAIAH 55:12

Some days, Lord, things are going so well that it
feels like all of creation is singing Your praises, and
I join with them. Other days, even when creation
sings, I don't feel like praising. Thank You, Lord,
for the reminder from the mountains and trees that
no matter what today brings, You promise me joy.
Help me to live out Your joy every day.

Amen

(Agreement in Prayer)

When we are done with praying, we automatically say the word *amen*. We often treat this small word as though it were the "good-bye" we mutter at the end of a phone conversation. We use it to say in effect, "Signing off now, God. I'm going back to my life, and I'll talk to You later."

But this ancient Hebrew word actually means something quite different. It is a way to seal the truth of what we have just prayed. It expresses our wholehearted commitment to our prayer, our total agreement. Heart, mind, and body, we surrender ourselves to God's answer to our prayer.

Let It Be

*And Mary said, Behold the handmaid of
the Lord; be it unto me according to thy word.*
LUKE 1:38

Lord, help me to follow Mary's example when
she found out that she was pregnant with the
Son of God. Her world was rocked, God! What
a scandal! A good Jewish girl pregnant before she
was married? Unthinkable! But she accepted the
news and surrendered her life and her body to Your
will. Help me to accept Your word, no matter what
it says to me, and surrender myself to it.

Right Motives

Ye ask, and receive not, because ye ask amiss,
that ye may consume it upon your lusts.
JAMES 4:3

*G*od, I admit that sometimes I am guilty of
treating my prayers as a wish list to a Santa-God.
Or maybe I treat You as though You were a vending
machine—if I say the right words in the right
order, I'll get what I want. If I'm honest, I know
that selfishness and greed may slip into a request
here or there. Today I ask that You show me when
my prayers are corrupted by selfish desires. Give me
pure motives, a pure heart, and a clear conscience.

Confidence

And this is the confidence that we have in him, that, if we ask any thing according to his will, he heareth us.
1 JOHN 5:14

As I pray, Lord, I rest in the confidence that You are always listening and that You understand the thoughts behind my prayers, even when I cannot. I am never speaking into empty air! Thank You for the confidence I also experience through the power of Your Holy Spirit that lives inside my heart. With You on my side, I can accomplish much for Your Kingdom!

The Truth

Jesus saith unto him, I am the way, the truth, and the life: no man cometh unto the Father, but by me.
JOHN 14:6

When I pray to You, God, I pray in Your Son's name. He is the way, He is the truth, and He will show me the way to You so that I can live the life that You intend for me. Help me to not be distracted by other false paths that may seem attractive or easier. Make my journey one that invites others to follow me, just as I follow Christ.

United in Prayer

*I say unto you, That if two of you shall agree on earth
as touching any thing that they shall ask, it shall be
done for them of my Father which is in heaven.*
MATTHEW 18:19

Thank You, Lord, for others who share my faith
in You. Thank You for the privilege of praying
with them, for worshipping with them, for
working together to build Your Kingdom. Thank
You that when we pray together, You hear us and
that when we gather together, You are there with
us. Help us to be the living, breathing, and active
body of Christ that we are meant to be.

Abiding

If ye abide in me, and my words abide in you, ye shall ask what ye will, and it shall be done unto you.
JOHN 15:7

Father, help me to abide in You as I pray—not quickly spitting out my requests and then dwelling on my worries and woes. Keep my thoughts focused on You as I wait for Your answers to my prayers, no matter how soon You answer them. Keep me close and allow me to abide in You as You ultimately answer my requests, and give me the peace of knowing that You work all things for good.

Wavering Hearts

Let him ask in faith, nothing wavering.
For he that wavereth is like a wave of the
sea driven with the wind and tossed.
JAMES 1:6

*Y*ou know how easily my heart wavers and
wobbles, Lord. I'm like a boat that's out in open
water, the world's woes tossing me around like
high waves. Take the helm of my boat, I pray.
And then after I've given over control of the
vessel, quiet the wind and waves. Help me to
pray with faith's absolute calm, knowing that
You have already ordained the outcome and
that You have my best interest at heart.

Anything!

For verily I say unto you, That whosoever shall say unto this mountain, Be thou removed, and be thou cast into the sea; and shall not doubt in his heart, but shall believe that those things which he saith shall come to pass; he shall have whatsoever he saith.

MARK 11:23

I don't want to throw any mountains into the ocean, God—and it's hard for me to believe that Jesus really meant what He said here. Show me the truth of His words. Teach me to pray according to Your will.

Power

*The effectual fervent prayer of a
righteous man availeth much.*
JAMES 5:16

Sometimes I say, "The only thing I can do
now is pray." I mean that I've done everything
I could think to do, and now as a last resort,
I'll fall back on prayer. Forgive me, Father, for
trusting in things that are not from You and for
setting my mind on worldly things. Remind me
that prayer is never the last resort and that You
are faithful in hearing it. Teach me to see the
power that prayer can unleash in the world.

In All My Ways

---

*In all thy ways acknowledge him,
and he shall direct thy paths.*
PROVERBS 3:6

God, I claim Your presence in each aspect of my life. Thank You for Your steadfast love and abounding grace. I honor You alone with my successes and acknowledge Your guiding hand on my life. Help me to set my eyes only on You. Teach me what it is to trust You with all my heart and to not lean on my own wisdom or understanding. May my heart always seek to bring glory to Your name and may my prayers always reflect this reality.

Willing Mind

Know thou the God of thy father, and serve him
with a perfect heart and with a willing mind:
for the LORD searcheth all hearts, and understandeth
all the imaginations of the thoughts: if thou
seek him, he will be found of thee.
1 CHRONICLES 28:9

*M*ake my mind willing, Lord. Help me to trust
that Your plans for me are better than the plans I
have for myself. Place Your desires in my heart, that
I may be able to walk fully in Your will for my life.
Help me to agree with Your ways for my life. I seek
You who understands me completely.

Perfect Heart

*Let your heart therefore be perfect with the LORD
our God, to walk in his statutes, and to keep his
commandments, as at this day.*
1 KINGS 8:61

*Y*ou know I can never achieve perfection on
my own, Lord God. But I surrender my heart to
You absolutely. Keep my heart and mind from
wandering and allow me to remain true only to
You. I thank You for Your never-ending grace that
sustains my life and that You never leave me or
forsake me. Through my prayer, I commit myself
totally to You and Your law for my life.

Willing

*I know also, my God, that thou triest the heart,
and hast pleasure in uprightness. As for me,
in the uprightness of mine heart I have
willingly offered all these things.*
1 CHRONICLES 29:17

I give You, God, everything I have to offer,
willingly and gladly. I know that everything I have
You have provided and have entrusted to me. Give
me a whole heart to follow after You and keep
Your commandments. Keep forever in my heart
Your purposes and thoughts. Show me anything I
am holding back. I want You to have it all.

Truthful Heart

*Lord, who shall abide in thy tabernacle?
who shall dwell in thy holy hill? He that
walketh uprightly, and worketh righteousness,
and speaketh the truth in his heart.*
PSALM 15:1–2

Lord, sometimes I lie to myself. Sometimes I try to lie to You. But You know me. You know my thoughts before I think them. Reveal to me Your truth, so that my prayers may be true, righteous, and upright. Show me how to live a blameless life.

One Mind

*That ye may with one mind and one mouth glorify
God, even the Father of our Lord Jesus Christ.*
ROMANS 15:6

Unite me in prayer with others, Father God. Let
no division come between us as we talk with You.
Give me patience in dealing with people who aren't
exactly like me and can be trying; remind me that
patience will build up Your Church. Forgive me for
any gossip or malicious words I've spoken against
my brothers and sisters and give me a heart that
longs for their good. Bring to my mind ways I can
show love that will bring more glory to You.

Believing

Be not faithless, but believing.
JOHN 20:27

I believe in You, Jesus. I believe in Your power and wisdom and love. I believe that Your atoning work on the cross has washed me of all my unrighteousness and that through it, I stand in perfect righteousness before God. Take my life— all my words and deeds—and use them for Your glory. Teach me to trust You, not requiring proof as Thomas did, but believing You at Your Word alone. Thank You that Your Word is truth and brings life to me and to those around me.

Scripture Index

UL 5 Peter popoff

1.800-925-5528
U M
miracle spring water